Haunting Tales of Haworth

Nestled deep in the heart ʊ
quaint little town of Haworth, known for its picturesque
countryside, charming cobbled streets and the literary
legacy of the world-famous Bronte sisters. But beneath
the idyllic surface of this serene town lies a darker,
more sinister history that has given rise to some of the
most chilling ghost stories in England. From haunted
mansions to cursed alleyways, from spectral figures to
headless horsemen, Haworth is a place where the veil
between the living and the dead is thin, and the
supernatural is never far away. In this book, we will
delve into the most popular old ghost stories of
Haworth, uncovering the spine-tingling tales of the
spirits that still haunt this historic town, and exploring
the mysteries and legends that have kept generations of
locals and visitors alike on the edge of their seats. So,
turn down the lights, settle in for a spooky journey
through the ghostly heart of Haworth, and prepare to
be chilled to the bone as we delve into the most
terrifying stories of the supernatural in this quaint little
town

**15 of the most popular
old ghost stories in Haworth, West Yorkshire:**

1. The Ghostly Tale of Top Withens: The haunted farmhouse that served as the inspiration for Wuthering Heights, the classic novel by Emily Bronte.

2. The Apparition of the Grey Lady: The tragic tale of a woman who died in childbirth and whose ghost still haunts the hallways of an old mansion in Haworth.

3. The Phantom of the Black Bull: A ghostly figure that is said to roam the upper floors of an old coaching inn in Haworth, leaving behind an icy chill and an eerie sense of unease.

4. The Headless Horseman of Stanbury: A spectral figure on horseback, galloping through the village of Stanbury and instilling terror in anyone who sets eyes on him.

5. The Screaming Skull of Bridgehouse Beck: A cursed skull that was kept hidden in a barn near Haworth and is said to shriek whenever it is disturbed.

6. The Ghostly Bride of Thornton: A woman who died on her wedding day and whose ghost still wanders the corridors of an old hall in Thornton.

7. The Phantom Coach of Oxenhope: A ghostly carriage that is said to race through the streets of Oxenhope, driven by a headless coachman and pulled by four black horses.

8. The Lady in Blue: The ghost of a woman who died of a broken heart and whose spirit still inhabits the ruins of an old abbey in Haworth.

9. The Specter of Haworth Parsonage: The ghostly presence that is felt by visitors to the parsonage where the Bronte sisters lived and wrote their famous novels.

10. The White Lady of Ponden Hall: A spectral figure in white that is said to haunt the rooms of this ancient hall near Haworth.

11. The Spooklight of Keighley Road: A mysterious light that has been reported by many motorists driving

along Keighley Road, said to be a supernatural phenomenon.

12. The Haunted Alleyway of Haworth: A narrow alleyway that is said to be cursed and haunted by the ghosts of the people who were buried alive there during the plague.

13. The Ghosts of Weavers' Square: The spectral figures that are said to appear in this historic square on certain nights, leaving behind a sense of dread and unease.

14. The Curse of Haworth Church: The strange occurrences and ghostly happenings that have been reported at the church in Haworth, believed to be the result of a curse placed on it centuries ago.

15. The Poltergeist of Lumb Bank: A malevolent spirit that is said to be responsible for moving objects and causing disturbances in this historic mansion near Haworth.

1. The Ghostly Tale of Top Withens: The haunted farmhouse that served as the inspiration for Wuthering Heights, the classic novel by Emily Bronte.

On the lonely and misty moors of Haworth, sits a farmhouse known throughout the world under the name of Top Withens. The tumbledown structure, surrounded by a rocky hillside and surrounded by a desolate landscape, is a source of fascination and dread for visitors from all over the world. The house was the inspiration for one of literature's most iconic Gothic novels, Wuthering Heights, written by the English writer, Emily Bronte. There are strange and eerie stories associated with Top Withens. Stories of ghosts, apparitions, and unexplainable happenings. The following article examines the supposed ghostly tales surrounding the building and the surrounding moors.

Top Withens - The house said to have inspired the classic novel Wuthering Heights. Heaven knows there is enough drama and mystery surrounding this withered old farmstead, solemnly brooding on its hillside amidst the lonely West Yorkshire moors. Emily Bronte, the home-grown literary legend and author of Wuthering

Heights was familiar with the tale of the eerie house and the strange happenings associated with it. The farmhouse was deemed to be the inspiration for the iconic character of Heathcliff and the dark and brooding tale that eventually became known as Emily's most renowned masterpiece.

But what is the truth hidden behind the tale of Top Withens? Do the spirits of Heathcliff and his beloved Cathy still prowl these lonely moors at night waiting to fulfill their cursed love across lifetimes? Are the stories handed down through oral tradition and later immortalized in the pages of Wuthering Heights true? Or are they merely fanciful fiction spun for the purpose of terrorizing the squeamish?

While some may dismiss such tales as mere superstition or folklore, many others believe that there is a true supernatural presence lurking within the walls of Top Withens farmhouse. Numerous intriguing stories circulate among the locals in the area concerning Top Withens and the eerie occurrences that have taken place there over the years.

One of the most famous stories connected with Top Withens involves a man named Earnshaw, the original owner of the house who was said to have two children, a son, and a daughter. While Earnshaw was away on a business trip, his children discovered an abandoned, sickly-looking boy on the moors. The boy was taken in, and upon his recovery the Earnshaw children's discovered that his name was Heathcliff. The story tells us that a bitter enmity developed between Heathcliff and the Earnshaw son due to his father's affection toward the strange boy. Meanwhile, a love triangle between Heathcliff and the Earnshaw children's daughter Catherine that eventually devolved into tragedy became the plot of Wuthering Heights. The extent to which this story is true or fictional is lost to time.

The eerie farmhouse itself is barren and lifeless, with nothing standing in the way of the moors' relentless winds and storms. It's said that the winds on Emily Bronte's final journey to the house were so strong that she had difficulty standing. Visitors to Top Withens can easily picture the scenes of Wuthering Heights while gazing out from the exact location that Bronte had stood from while penning the novel. The archetypal moody Yorkshire landscape around portray the settings she so vividly narrated in the book.

However, in spite of their beauty, those same winds and hills are what threaten the farmhouse with extinction. Today, visitors to Top Withens are met with only scattered rubble - the remains of the farmhouse that has been ruined by time and the weather over the years. It is said, however, that this very same ruin holds the memories and the remnants of the eerie occurrences of the past, waiting behind the thin veil of reality that makes one's hair stand on end.

The area surrounding Top Withens has been the site of strange and unexplainable events, and the stories and legends that are associated with it always make visitors shiver in fascination and dread. People have reported mysterious whispers and inexplicable noises coming from the ruined farmhouse. Others claim that they have been followed by 'icy fingers' which clutched their necks without warning. The doors and windows of the farmhouse have been said to move on their own, as if guided by invisible entities. A visitor once described a strong and horrible smell that permeated the air during their visit to Top Withens, almost as if an unseen force was trying to mask their movements with the smell.

But perhaps the most disturbing tale associated with Top Withens are the stories of ghostly apparitions seen on the moors at night. People have reported sightings of a strange, spectral figure on the moors surrounding the farmhouse, a figure that disappears just as suddenly as it appears, appearing and disappearing without any apparent source. Some have even claimed to have encountered this ghostly figure while touring the farmhouse, only to have the apparition vanish before their eyes.

There are many stories that surround this eerie farmhouse that inspired one of the most famous books of all time,

Here's 2 of mine

1ST STORY

As darkness fell over the moors of Haworth, the village's ancient Abbey stood out in the autumn night sky like an ominous specter. The moors themselves, still and silent, wrapped in a haze and an early autumn chill that sunk into the bones of all who wandered through. It was here that the lonely farmhouse of Top Withens lay.

The old, tumbledown structure was nestled amongst the rocky hillside. It was a building which was said to hold a dark and ghostly secret. Emily Bronte, the renowned author of Wuthering Heights, was said to have visited Top Withens and been inspired by the foreboding nature of the farmhouse and the surrounding moors. From these tales, one can imagine what the abandoned farmhouse must have been like in the novel.

The farmhouse was once a cheerful place, with a lively family residing within its walls. But now, the only sound that echoed through the empty halls of the farmhouse was the rustling of leaves and the mournful howling of the wind. The farmhouse had been battered by the elements over the years, its walls crumbled and its roof cracked. The eerie silence was disturbed only by the odd tinkling of broken glass, a clue to the reality of it having been abandoned for many years.

It was in this setting that three friends, John, Emily, and Mary found themselves one dark and stormy night. They had decided to go on a ghost hunt, and Top Withens was their chosen location for this eerie task. They had brought along their flashlights, some other essential equipment, and, of course, a good deal of courage.

They parked their car on the side of the deserted and lonely Haworth road, then hiked through the dense and chilly moorland. Along the way, they came across an old shepherd's cottage, but they dismissed it as too small to be of interest and ventured further. The winds picked up, and rain began to fall hard and cold on their hoods and jackets.

Finally, the outline of the farmhouse came into view through the pouring rain. It was an unwelcoming sight, a ruined relic of a long bygone age, with the overwhelming sense of spookiness growing as they approached it. They arrived at the farmhouse's entrance and gingerly pushed open the creaking door. With a loud groan, the door swung open, causing the rusted hinges to shriek with the wind's help. The trio shone their flashlights into the dark and the empty abyss, but there was nothing visible in the flickering beams.

The old farmhouse appeared to them like an abandoned stage set, its furniture and family belongings smashed or exiled by time and gravity. As they walked through the old house, their flashlights caught a glimmer of something shiny. They approached, curious, only to find a rusted and battered old frame hanging on the wall.

The picture was of a young woman, draped in the clothes of another era, her eyes and expression swept by sadness. Beneath the picture, there was a tag that read "Cathy Earnshaw." Emily recognized the name immediately. Cathy Earnshaw was the heroine of Wuthering Heights, the young woman who, in the novel, forms a forbidden relationship with the enigmatic Heathcliff. The frame was a testament to the eerie legacy of the house and its connection to the Bronte sisters.

John and Mary were not keen to linger in this spooky and forsaken place, they had heard too many ghost tales of Top Withens, and Emily agreed that a hasty retreat would be the best course of action. But as they turned, Emily caught a glimpse of something out of the corner of her eye, something strange and unsettling.

Emily gasped as she spun around, her flashlight sweeping the rooms, searching for the source of the movement. In one of the empty rooms, she caught sight of something that sent a chill down her spine. There was something there, moving amidst the gloom. Something was scuttling around the borders of the room, but the light from their torches failed to catch it.

Emily whispered to her friends, "Can you see that?" pointing towards the corner of the room. "It's like something's moving there, in the shadows." But her friends saw nothing, and they soon departed, convinced that Emily was merely imagining things.

As they trudged back through the moorland surrounding the farmhouse, they had no idea that they were being followed. A faint whisper on the wind followed them, joined by the mournful howling of the sturdy moors in the distance. Meanwhile, the eerie old house remained poised and haunted, watching over the lonely and desolate moorland with its dark secrets.

Top Withens remains a chilling and forbidding location, seeming like it's from another era, haunted by the ghosts of the past that Emily Bronte and countless others have immortalized in their tales. Its ruined walls seem to whisper stories of lost love and tragic heartbreak, and, in the darkness of night,

2ND STORY

Nestled in the heart of the foreboding Yorkshire moors, Top Withens stood alone; a weather-beaten relic of a time long past. It was an old and haunted house that lay abandoned on the moors, a place shrouded in mystery and tragedy. Cartloads of rumors and whispered stories had surrounded the eerie house for centuries, tales of ghosts haunting its halls and roaming the surrounding moors.

Few brave souls dared to venture to the farmhouse, and those who did soon regretted it. It was rumored that even the local villagers avoided the house during the darkest nights. They knew not what lurked within its desolate walls, but they felt an inexplicable fear that seemed to emanate from the very foundations of the house.

One night, a group of teenagers, skeptical and daring, arrived at the foot of the haunted farmhouse with a plan to unlock the secrets that lay within. They had been fascinated by the stories of the mysterious events that took place around the old building for many years. Even their parents, the elders of the village, had grown up with the tales of the eerie figures who roamed the moors, the ones that supposedly waited to lure unsuspecting travelers to their doom.

The five teens huddled together, their hearts pounding as they pushed open the creaking, wooden door that led inside. They were greeted by a musty odor, a foul mix of damp earth and rotting wood that filled the chilly autumn air. The floors were covered in dirt and debris, the walls were picking apart, and the light from their torches seemed to flicker and dance erratically across the endless empty rooms.

Whispers echoed off the walls of the old building, and shadows seemed to follow their every move. The teens tried to laugh it off, but a deep and unexplainable fear had taken hold of them.

As they continued to explore the abandoned rooms of the farmhouse, they could not shake the feeling of being watched. The whispers and shadows grew more insistent, until finally, one of the teens cried out, "Do you guys hear that?"

"What?" asked the others, shuffling closer together.

"That whispering," whispered the first who had spoken, pointing at the shadows in the corner of the room - motionless and yet still prominent.

The other teens listened closely, and they could hear the sound of voices, murmuring low in an unknown language too incomprehensible for them to understand. Their torches flickered and shone on the frozen shadows of the corner, but nothing was there to greet them.

Suddenly, there was a loud creak, and then a thud. One of the kids had stumbled, knocking over a heavy wooden chair that was left to rot on the old wood floor.

The other teens turned to investigate, and as they approached the youth who had stumbled, they noticed that something was amiss. His face was pale and clammy, and his eyes were wide and terrified. He stammered, trying to get the words out, but all he could manage was, "something- something just touched me."

A dark thrill ran through all of them, but dread mixed with that sensation when it became painfully obvious that the teen was not joking. The room grew suddenly colder. Their breaths were visible in the air, and hair began to prickle at the back of their necks.

In silence, they crept away, leaving the old building behind with hopes of making it to their homes. But something followed them.

They had walked for several minutes before the teen who had been touched let out a shriek, running in fear and pain. He clutched at his forehead, an ominous cut running jaggedly over his left eye, quickly swelling and dripping red.

The other teens ran to him, demanding to know if he was ok, but he could only whimper and point in the direction of the old farmhouse.

The teens could not believe their eyes - a dark figure was emerging from the abandoned building, beckoning them over with long, bony fingers. As the figure approached them, tendrils of smoke twisted and coiled around it, obscuring its features. But the eyes. The eyes blazed like coals, inviting them closer.

The teens stood frozen in terror, no longer daring to approach or plead to whatever had entered this world through the abandoned farmhouse. They were powerless to stop it as it suddenly surged forward, its inhuman voice screeching in anger and delight as it enveloped them.

From that day forward, the abandoned farmhouse of Top Withens stood as a warning to all those foolish enough to dare to step inside. The stories of hauntings and specters once hushed in ghostly tales and whispered rumors now became a reality and a warning to all who tread those lonely moors.

2. The Apparition of the Grey Lady: The tragic tale of a woman who died in childbirth and whose ghost still haunts the hallways of an old mansion in Haworth.

Deep in the heart of West Yorkshire, surrounded by rolling green hills and dense woodlands sits an old mansion known as Haworth Hall. This majestic building is a hidden gem, a place that hides many dark secrets and mysterious tales. And one such story is the tale of the Grey Lady.

She was once a beautiful woman, so beautiful that many people would stop and stare when she walked through the village. Her beauty faded over time but even now, in death, she remains the epitome of what a woman should be. Her hair is long and silver, the lace of her gown is pristine, and her skin is as pale as moonlight.

The Grey Lady's true story is one of tragedy. She was the wife of a wealthy man who had given her everything she could desire, but unfortunately, she longed for something more - a child. She prayed and wished with everything she had, but her body was not able to conceive. Finally, she became pregnant, and she was ecstatic, but her joy was short-lived. The delivery was difficult, and the baby was stillborn. The Grey Lady died not long after, leaving behind only her grieving husband and a place for her in the Hall's many ghostly tales.

The residents of the mansion had long known her ghostly presence, made manifest through the mists of time that shrouded the place. They tell of an apparition that they see in the corridors, drifting silently and gracefully across the length of Haworth Hall. Her ghostly figure is sometimes seen in photographs taken of the building and its surroundings - a spectral presence that both frightens and amazes those who witness it.

The Grey Lady is usually found in the main hall's upstairs dressing room, where she once spent many hours preparing herself for social engagements. The dressing room is still filled with all the Victorian-era dressings, from corsets and bustles to lace collars and silken gowns, turning the room into a time capsule befitting the era in which she lived.

Many have reported seeing her wandering around the upstairs corridors, dressed in her beloved gown, spinning a music box or a locket, as if lost in thought. Others have described nighttime encounters with her ethereal figure. Visitors to the mansion catch a glimpse of the Grey Lady standing beside the bed, staring at them with sad, mournful eyes. Whatever be the manner in which it happens, all who've seen her have been shocked to find that the woman who looked so real had lacked one essential trait- that of breathing.

Over the years, the presence of the Grey Lady has been a source of comfort and intrigue for those who believe in ghosts and spirits. Those who visit the mansion pay homage to her haunting presence, but some visitors cannot help but feel a sense of unease when wandering the corridors at night. There are those who feel her cold breath on their cheeks, and others who swear they've seen her ghostly figure when walking the gardens.

Despite the ghosts and apparitions that roam the building's halls, Haworth Hall remains a testament to the expertise and perseverance of those long gone. However, the Grey Lady remains the most striking of all the specters that haunt the place, a symbol of love and tragedy. It is the story of the Grey Lady that persists, surviving throughout generations, reminding us that death cannot snuff out the eternal beauty that lies in true love - even when it is followed by tragedy.

2 OF MY STORYS
1ST STORY

Haworth Old Hall was a place where fear and horror roamed free. Once a grand and beautiful mansion, the halls now lay dark and foreboding, a place where time stood still, and the secrets that resided within were never meant to see the light of day.

The Grey Lady haunted the halls of Haworth Old Hall, her soul trapped between the realms of the living and the dead. She roamed the corridors, a ghostly apparition that left a trail of whispers and shadows in her wake. Over the years, many had attempted to uncover the mystery of her tragic past and the reasons for her supernatural return, but all had failed, falling to the trap of her seductive presence instead.

It all started when a group of friends decided to spend the night in the abandoned mansion. Curiosity had gotten the better of them, and despite the warnings of the locals, they ventured forth into the dark and musty halls. They were soon gripped with a sense of unease, as if they were being watched, even though they were alone.

The group split up, each taking a different turn in the labyrinthine hallways. They knew that it was only a matter of time before they encountered something that would shatter their illusions and push them to the edge of terror.

It was the sound of a music box that first alerted them to the presence of the Grey Lady. The shrill and haunting melody echoed through the halls, sending shivers down their spines. As they approached the source of the sound, they could see her spectral figure, spinning the music box in the center of the room.

Suddenly the music stopped and the Grey Lady turned towards them. She looked directly into their eyes, and they could see the sheer, unadulterated horror in her expression. Her face twisted in agony as she screamed, a blood-curdling cry that pierced the darkness.

The friends ran in terror, trying to escape the grasping tendrils of the Grey Lady's curse. But the hallways seemed to shift and change, forcing them deeper into the heart of the mansion. Every corner they turned led them deeper into the maze of horrors that awaited them.

As the night wore on, they could hear the Lady's terrible sobs, a forlorn wail that filled the halls with an air of sadness and despair. They tried to leave, to escape the hellish mansion, but their way was blocked by the Lady's spectral presence. And as they turned to flee, they caught a glimpse of a woeful, ghostly baby, draped in swaddling clothes, that whispered in the Grey Lady's ear...

The friends were never seen again. They say that the Grey Lady still haunts the halls of Haworth Old Hall, calling out for her lost child, and seeking revenge against those who dared to disturb her eternal rest. The mansion now lays in ruin, a symbol of the horrors that lie hidden beneath its walls. And those brave enough to venture inside without fear leave only with unyielding terror as their travel companion - for the Grey Lady does not allow strangers to leave her realm unscathed.

The sun was setting over Haworth Old Hall, casting a crimson glow over the ivy-covered walls. Lily, a young girl with curious eyes, stood by the wrought-iron gates that led up to the mansion. She had heard stories of the Grey Lady, but like all children, she was brave and unafraid of the supernatural.

She had snuck away from her parents and had been wandering the gardens when she saw her - a woman wrapped in a long, flowing grey gown, a faint aura of energy emanating from her. Lily was not afraid; instead, she was fascinated and felt drawn to investigate. She made her way to the entrance of the mansion and pushed open the door, letting out a screeching sound that echoed through the rooms.

As she made her way inside, the creaking floorboards under her feet, she could hear a sound coming from upstairs, like the soft humming of a tune. She walked up the winding staircase, her small feet tapping against the wooden steps. The sound grew louder as she climbed, and as she entered the upstairs hallway, she saw the ghostly figure of the Grey Lady.

The Lady was spinning a music box, her eyes fixed on the floor, lost in thought. Lily stared in amazement at the ethereal beauty that stood before her. Suddenly, the Lady lifted her piercing silver eyes and looked directly at her, a longing and mournful gaze in her eyes.

Lily, caught off guard, stepped back in terror and stumbled down the stairs. She ran from the haunted mansion, her heart racing like a locomotive's steam engine. She made it to the gate and turned back one last time. Looking at the eerie mansion, she could hear a sad, forlorn wail, the sound of a woman's soul crying out in despair.

From that day on, Lily was changed. She could never shake the feeling of unease that had been implanted in her soul, an overwhelming fear of the supernatural and the unknown. She knew that the Grey Lady still haunted the halls of Haworth Old Hall, calling out for her lost child and seeking revenge against those who dared to disturb her eternal rest.

Years later, Lily returned to the haunted mansion. She had overcome her fears, had faced the unknown and come back alive. She climbed the winding stairs once again, this time to the room where the Grey Lady had been spinning the music box. And there, sitting on the dusty floor, was the same music box, its haunting tune still echoing through the halls.

Lily realized what she must do. She wound up the music box and spun it around. Then, with tears streaming down her face, she sang a mournful lullaby, a song the Grey Lady had sung to her child so very long ago. As Lily sang, the Grey Lady's ghostly figure appeared, standing beside her once again.

The Grey Lady listened, her eyes shut tight in pain and then, she began to fade away, the music and the ghosts memories disappearing with her. Lily knew that she had done something good, had given the Grey Lady some closure. She never forgot the haunting memory of Haworth Old Hall, but she felt a sense of relief, for the Grey Lady and herself.

3. The Phantom of the Black Bull: A ghostly figure that is said to roam the upper floors of an old coaching inn in Haworth, leaving behind an icy chill and an eerie sense of unease.

The Phantom of the Black Bull was a ghostly presence that roamed the upper floors of the old coaching inn in Haworth. Those who had encountered the Phantom spoke of its icy chill, which left them trembling with an unexplainable sense of terror and unease.

The Black Bull Inn was already known for its dark and haunting history. Built in the 17th century, the place has seen countless tragedies and horrors. But the Phantom added a whole new level of terror to the place. People would hear footfalls outside their rooms, doors creaking open, and then the sound of a heavy and raspy breathing. When they opened the doors, they would find nothing but a cold draught that seemed to snake through the hallways.

Legend says that the Phantom was once a guest who had died in one of the rooms upstairs. The inn was bustling with visitors at the time, and nobody had noticed his death until days later. His body was found, lifeless and cold, in one of the rooms on the upper floor. The staff tried to cover up the death, but rumors spread, and the Phantom was born.

Since that fateful day, the Phantom's ghostly presence had been felt by guests and staff members alike. His ghostly aura would lead travelers on a haunting journey through the dark corridors of the inn's upper floors, never quite disappearing, leaving behind an icy chill that would linger in the air for hours.

The Phantom was known to have a temper, his angry spirit lashing out at those who dared to disturb his eternal slumber. He would move furniture, slam doors shut, and even throw objects at unsuspecting victims. There were rumors of a secret chamber where the Phantom's restless spirit dwelt, a place of utter darkness where the shadows seemed to come alive.

Eventually, the inn fell into disrepair, the dark and haunted halls of the Black Bull now silent and abandoned. But the stories of the Phantom persisted, his ghostly presence still felt by those who dared to explore the inn after nightfall.

The Phantom of the Black Bull remains one of the most notorious and feared ghosts of Haworth. His spirit still roams the halls and corridors of the old inn that he once called home. Beware those who venture into its dark and ruined rooms, for the Phantom's presence still looms large and his icy chill remains a warning of the horrors that lie in wait.

HERES MY TWO STORYS
1ST STORY

It was a dark and stormy night in Haworth. The rain was beating against the windows, and the wind was howling like a pack of wolves. In the heart of the town stood the Black Bull Inn, standing tall, resolute, and unyielding against the fierce elements and the chilling cold of the night.

Gabe, an adventurous traveler, had just arrived in town and needed a place to stay for the night. He had heard the rumors about the haunting of the Black Bull Inn but was undaunted by the tales. Gabe had always been a skeptic regarding the supernatural. He had always believed in the power of science, logic, and reason. He looked forward to staying at the historic inn, convinced that the stories were nothing more than tales spun by the superstitious locals.

As soon as he entered, the pub's warmth soothed his chilled skin. The wood paneling and the simple decor registered in his mind. Gabe exchanged pleasantries with the innkeeper, Joe, before making his way up the stairs to his room. As he ascended the stairs, he couldn't help but glance at the dimly lit hallway that led to the upper floors.

The atmosphere in the hallway was heavier and more ominous. Gabe could feel a chill run down his spine as he read the room numbers along the corridor. He finally pushed open the door to his room and paused to take in the surroundings.

The room was small, but it smelled clean and well kept. There were a few oil paintings on the wall, a small desk, a chair, and a bed. A window looked out over the town center and afforded a good view. Gabe smiled to himself and chuckled at his fleeting unease. He convinced himself that there was nothing to fear and settled down to read.

As the night wore on, the storm outside grew fiercer. Gabe felt increasingly uneasy, unable to shake the feeling that someone was watching him. His mind turned to the rumors of the ghostly Phantom. He wondered if the ghost of the former guest was, in fact, real and if he was already present on the upper floors of the inn.

Gabe's fears were soon justified when he heard strange noises outside his door. He opened it cautiously and saw nothing but darkness, silence greeting him. Then, he noticed that the door to the neighboring room was ajar, a pale and ghostly light emanating from within. Gabe moved slowly towards the light.

As he drew closer, the light flickered, illuminating the room for a brief moment. Gabe saw a shadowy figure perched by the bed, a figure that seemed almost otherworldly. Gabe's curiosity piqued, and he pushed the door slightly, trying to get a better look.

As if sensing his presence, the figure moved. It was humanoid, with horns and glowing eyes that pierced the darkness. Gabe gasped and stumbled back in terror, his heart pounding against his chest. Somewhere in the distance, he could hear a low and menacing sound, like a growl.

Gabe knew he had to flee the room, his instincts kicking in as he rushed through the hallway, trying to escape the otherworldly presence. The corridors twisted and turned, leading him on a haunted journey that seemed to last forever. He saw things that chilled him to the bone - an old, rusted scissors lying on the floor, a door slowly creaking open as if to invite him in, and a portrait on the wall that seemed to come alive and smile at him.

He could hear laughter and whispers, but nobody was there. The cold air stung as if soaked with the taste of death and decay. Gabe knew that he wasn't alone - there was a supernatural presence that seemed to follow him, watching his every move.

Suddenly, he saw a figure standing in front of him - a pale, ghostly apparition holding a music box. The phantom was surrounded by an ethereal glow that seemed to consume Gabe's very being. His limbs felt weak, and his vision blurred as the phantom took hold of his mind.

As quickly as it arrived, the ghostly presence vanished. Gabe reeled back, dazed and confused. He knew he had to escape, to get out of the inn before it was too late.

He stumbled down the flight of stairs, his breaths shallow and erratic.

As Gabe made his way towards the exit, he could sense the presence of a force, something that seemed to bear down upon him. He pushed on, propelled by the fear of the supernatural. He finally made it to the door, the rain lashing against him as he ran out into the night.

Back in his hometown, Gabe sought the help of a medium, someone who could help him make sense of the supernatural entity he had encountered. The medium listened to his story, nodding knowingly from time to time. She could sense the palpable fear that Gabe was experiencing.

The medium told Gabe that what he had

2ND STORY

The Black Bull Inn had been a hub for travelers, horse caravans, and curious minds since the 17th century. Its walls had seen laughter and merriment, but it also had seen the darker side of life. Being in a prime location to host smugglers, spies, and other nefarious activities, the inn had seen its share of bloodshed and pain.

It wasn't long before the locals began to hear rumors of a ghostly figure that roamed through the upper floors of the inn, leaving behind an icy chill and an eerie sense of unease. This entity had been given the name "The Phantom of the Black Bull." It was said to have been a former guest who died inside the inn and whose spirit remained restless in death.

Although the inn had fallen into disrepair, there were still people who dared to spend the night inside its broken walls. Some stayed for the story, while others stayed for the thrill of encountering something otherworldly. Most, however, never returned. These stories became legends passed down from generation to generation and kept the inn shrouded in mystery and fear.

Emily was one such curious traveler. She had heard the stories of the Phantom, and they had piqued her interest. Being a seasoned explorer of the supernatural, she decided to spend the night at the Black Bull Inn, determined to discover the truth behind the myth.

Emily had traveled from afar to reach the small town in the middle of nowhere. Her heart was beating fast in anticipation, and her palms were sweaty as she approached the door of the inn. She was a brave woman, but there was something about the Black Bull Inn that made her uneasy.

As she entered the inn, Emily could feel an inexplicable chill creeping down her spine. The inn was unwelcoming and, in some ways, foreboding. The wooden floors and walls creaked as she passed through the hallways. There was an eerie aura that lingered in every corner of the inn.

Emily stood before the door of her room, feeling anxious as she turned the doorknob and stepped inside. The room was simple and sparsely decorated, with a large four-poster bed dominating the center. The room was cold, and the ambiance was grim.

The rain outside was picking up, and the sound of the wind began to grow louder. Emily took out her camera and started taking pictures of the room to capture the essence of the place. Suddenly, there was a knock on the door. Emily jumped in surprise, dropping her camera on the bed.

She approached the door and opened it to find the innkeeper, a middle-aged man with a friendly face. He welcomed her and informed her that there was nothing to be afraid of, assuring her that the stories of the Phantom were nothing but hot air.

Emily wanted to believe him, fearing that the stories may have been exaggerated. But as he left the room, that feeling of unease returned – stronger than ever before.

Emily had decided to turn in for the night, hoping to get a good night's rest before embarking on her ghost hunt. As she lay on the bed, she could hear the sound of the wind outside and the occasional creaking of the walls. She willed herself to fall asleep but found it impossible. Every time she closed her eyes, she felt like someone was watching her, waiting to pounce.

Suddenly, she heard the sound of footsteps outside her door. She got up and walked to the door, peering through the keyhole, but there was nothing there. She shrugged it off, convinced that it was just her imagination running wild.

Hours passed, and Emily was wide awake. Her mind raced as she tried to make sense of the strange noises and creaking floorboards outside. Then she heard something new, something chilling. It was the sound of a music box, its haunting tune echoing through the halls.

Emily felt her heart race and knew that she had to investigate. She dressed quickly and left the room, her feet padding softly on the wood floor as she made her way through the hallways in the direction of the sound.

As she drew closer to the room where the music box was playing, a chill ran down her spine. She could feel the presence of something dark and malevolent lurking in the shadows, and a sense of unease crept over her.

Emily pushed open the door and saw a pale, ghostly figure spinning the music box on a table. The entity was vaguely humanoid, but its features were distorted and twisted. It had slimy skin that appeared to be rotting, and its eyes were glowing orbs of pulsating light.

Emily approached the entity cautiously, her heart pounding in her throat. The entity turned to face her, and she could see the malevolence in its glowing eyes. She suddenly realized that she had made a terrible mistake, and she tried to run, but she was too late.

It was like the entity was waiting for her, and it seized her. Its ethereal grip was icy and painful. Emily

4. The Headless Horseman of Stanbury: A spectral figure on horseback, galloping through the village of Stanbury and instilling terror in anyone who sets eyes on him.

The story of the Headless Horseman of Stanbury is one that has been passed down from generation to generation in the village. According to legend, the Headless Horseman was once a brave and valiant knight who fought in the Wars of the Roses. He was said to have been incredibly skilled with a sword and had gained the respect and admiration of his peers and the common folk.

One fateful day, while engaged in a battle with his enemies, the knight was struck on the head by a sword, severing it from his body. His body collapsed to the ground, lifeless, and his head was never found.

The villagers buried the knight's body in the cemetery with great reverence, believing that his noble and courageous spirit would live on, even in death. However, it wasn't long before people began to see a spectral figure on horseback galloping through the village, instilling terror in anyone who laid eyes upon him.

The Headless Horseman would appear out of nowhere, his horse's hooves pounding the earth as he galloped down the narrow, winding streets of the village. He was said to be dressed in full armor, his face hidden by the visor of his helmet, and his head was nowhere to be seen.

Those who caught glimpses of the Horseman would tremble with fear, for his presence was accompanied by an icy chill that seemed to seep into their very bones. Some said that the Horseman was a portent of doom, while others believed that he was seeking vengeance against those who had wronged him in life.

The Headless Horseman's appearances were sporadic, but they were said to increase in frequency during the autumn months. The villagers would huddle together in fear, locking their doors and windows, praying that the Horseman would not target them.

There were those who were brave enough to confront the Headless Horseman, but they were said never to return. Some said that the Horseman would capture his victims and take them away to his lair, while others believed that he would decapitate them with a sword in a gruesome fashion.

The village elders warned their children to stay away from the cemetery at night, for it was said that the Headless Horseman's spirit was bound to it. They also cautioned them against wandering the streets after dark, for who knew when the Horseman would choose to make his appearance.

There were also rumors that the Horseman had a particular hatred for those who dared to mock or disrespect him. For this reason, some of the villagers would leave offerings of food and drink at his grave, hoping to appease his restless spirit.

As the years passed, the legend of the Headless Horseman of Stanbury grew, becoming more twisted and macabre with each retelling. Some added that the Horseman's horse was also headless, while others incorporated tales of cursed weapons, black magic, and demonic possession.

Despite the attempts of the villagers to rationalize the myth of the Headless Horseman, the truth remained a mystery. Some people claimed to have seen him, while others dismissed him as nothing more than a figment of their imaginations.

But for those who had seen the Headless Horseman, there was no doubt that he was real. His aura of malevolence and terror was palpable, and his chilling presence would leave them quaking with fear for days to come.

The Headless Horseman of Stanbury remained an enigma, an elusive figure that haunted the village and its inhabitants. His legacy was one of fear and terror, and he was a reminder that even in death, vengeance and malevolence could still reign supreme.

MY STORY

1ST STORY

It was a dark and stormy night in the village of Stanbury. The wind howled through the narrow alleyways, and the rain beat down on the rooftops. The villagers huddled in their homes, hoping to wait out the storm in safety. But they knew that there was something far worse than the storm looming outside their doors.

The Headless Horseman had been seen roaming through the village again, his spectral form galloping through the streets on a black horse. His chilling presence instilled terror in anyone who set eyes on him. Mothers held their children tight, and even the bravest of men cowered in fear.

For years, the villagers had spoken of the Headless Horseman, but he had always remained elusive, a legend passed down from generation to generation. But now, he had returned, and he was as real as the storm that raged around them.

As evening turned to night, the villagers could hear the Horseman's horse as it pounded down the road. They could feel its vibrations through the floors of their homes, a foreboding that chilled them to the bone. The Horseman's arrival had been anticipated, but the villagers were still unprepared.

Suddenly, the doors of the village inn burst open, and a group of travelers stumbled inside, soaked through from the storm. They hurried to close the door behind them, not realizing that they had brought something far worse inside with them.

One of the travelers peered out the window and saw the Headless Horseman ride past on his horse. He let out a scream, and the other villagers huddled closer, their eyes wide with terror. The Headless Horseman had found them.

The Horseman's hooves pounded outside the door, and the travelers could hear his labored breathing. One of the villagers, a brave man named Robert, decided to confront the Horseman head-on. He grabbed a nearby lantern and stepped outside into the storm.

As Robert approached the Horseman, he could feel his own courage falter. The Horseman's armor glinted in the dim light of the lantern, and his glowing eyes bored into Robert's soul. But Robert did not back down. He stood his ground, ready to fight for his home and his people.

The Horseman raised his sword and charged at Robert, his horse snarling and foaming at the mouth. Robert swung his own sword, and a thunderous clash echoed through the village. The travelers could hear the sound of metal against metal, and the Horseman's unearthly screams as he fought against Robert.

But Robert was relentless, and although the Horseman was a formidable opponent, he fought with all his might. In the end, Robert emerged victorious, and the Headless Horseman's spectral form dissipated into the heavy rain.

The village of Stanbury was safe once again, and the travelers breathed a sigh of relief. Robert had saved them all from a terrifying fate, but they knew that the legend of the Headless Horseman would live on.

Even in death, the Horseman's presence had been felt, sending a shiver down the spine of anyone who dared to speak his name. The villagers knew that they would never forget the terror of that dark and stormy night, and that the legend of the Headless Horseman of Stanbury would continue to haunt them for generations to come.

2DN STORY

The village of Stanbury was a place shrouded in fear, for the legend of the Headless Horseman had been passed down for generations. No one knew where he came from or what he wanted, but all knew that he was not a figure to be trifled with. So when a group of out-of-towners arrived one day, they were immediately warned to stay in their rooms after dark.

Despite this warning, one of the travelers, a young woman named Sarah, decided to venture outside and explore the village. She had always been drawn to tales of the supernatural, and the Headless Horseman was no exception.

As she walked through the streets, she could feel the weight of the Horseman's legend bearing down on her. Every sound was magnified, every shadow elongated into something sinister. Despite herself, Sarah felt a thrill of excitement, and she pressed on.

As she rounded a corner, she saw him. The Headless Horseman was galloping through the village, his spectral form illuminated by the moonlight. Sarah gasped and backed up, but she could not tear her eyes away from the terrifying sight.

The Horseman stopped in front of her, and Sarah could feel his cold breath on her face. She wanted to scream, but no sound would come out. It was as if the Horseman had robbed her of her voice and her courage.

Slowly, the Horseman raised his sword, and Sarah knew that it was the end. But suddenly, a voice called out from behind her, and she turned to see a young man standing there, brandishing a sword of his own.

The Horseman charged at the young man, and Sarah could hear the clash of metal ringing through the air. She cowered behind a nearby tree, too terrified to move.

When it was all over, the young man emerged victorious. The Headless Horseman was gone, and Sarah was left alone in the night. She knew that she had witnessed something incredible, something that she would never forget as long as she lived.

As she made her way back to the village inn, she realized that the young man who had saved her was nowhere to be seen. She asked the villagers about him, and they looked at her in confusion. They had not seen any young man, they said. No one had come or gone from the village that night.

Sarah knew that she had been saved by something supernatural, something beyond explanation. She left the village the next day, knowing that she would never be the same again. But she also knew that the legend of the Headless Horseman of Stanbury would continue to live on, and that there were brave souls in the world who were willing to face their fears and confront the unknown, even at their own peril.

5. The Screaming Skull of Bridgehouse Beck: A cursed skull that was kept hidden in a barn near Haworth and is said to shriek whenever it is disturbed.

The legend of the Screaming Skull of Bridgehouse Beck was one of the oldest and most terrifying in all of Haworth. For centuries, the villagers had whispered about the cursed skull that was said to make the very ground shake with its unearthly shrieks.

Rumors about the skull had been passed down from generation to generation, but few dared to venture near the barn where it was said to be hidden. Those who did often returned shaken and pale, their eyes haunted by something that they could not put into words.

One dark and stormy night, a group of young men decided to test their courage and venture into the barn themselves. They had heard the tale many times before, but they dismissed it as nothing more than a frightening story meant to keep children in line.

As they approached the barn, they could hear a faint sound coming from inside. It was a low and mournful moan, but they dismissed it as nothing more than the wind whistling through the cracks in the old structure.

But as they got closer, the sound grew louder and more insistent. It was no longer a mere moan, but a series of guttural shrieks that shook the very foundation of the barn.

The young men hesitated for a moment, but their pride and machismo urged them on. They stepped inside the barn and saw the skull resting on a pile of hay in the corner.

As soon as they approached the skull, it began to shriek with increasing intensity, its sound bouncing off the walls and ringing through their ears. The young men tried to cover their ears, but the skull's screams were too powerful. Soon, they were caught in a trance-like state, unable to move or look away from the shrieking skull.

Hours passed, or maybe just minutes, the young men were unable to gauge the time passing as they stood there frozen in fear. The skull continued to scream, its sound amplifying to an ear-splitting level. The young men knew they had made a grave mistake, and that the myth of the skull was indeed real.

It wasn't until the sun began to rise that the skull's screams finally began to fade away, much to the relief of the young men. They stumbled out of the barn, shaken to their core and forever traumatized by the cursed skull's shrieks.

Years passed, and the barn was left abandoned, a monument to the terror of the Screaming Skull of Bridgehouse Beck. To this day, villagers whisper about the cursed object, reminding each other not to disturb the skull's final resting place, lest they be subject to its terrifying shrieks of agony.

My story

For years, the cursed skull of Bridgehouse Beck had been the source of fear and terror for the small village near Haworth. The legend of the skull had been passed down for generations, and its terrifying reputation preceded it.

No one knew where the skull had come from or why it was cursed, but all knew that it was best to leave it alone. Anyone who dared to disturb the skull would be subjected to its deafening shrieks, which could be heard for miles around.

One day, a group of thrill-seekers arrived in the village, eager to explore the dark and mysterious corners of

Haworth. They had heard the legend of the screaming skull and were intrigued by its reputation.

Despite the warnings of the villagers, the group headed to the abandoned barn where the skull was said to be hidden. They had equipped themselves with cameras and voice recorders, eager to capture evidence of the skull's power.

As soon as they entered the barn, they could feel the temperature drop, and an eerie feeling settled over them. They scanned the space with their cameras, but they saw nothing out of the ordinary. The skull, however, was nowhere to be found.

One member of the group spotted a small pile of bones in the corner of the barn, and on closer inspection, they found the skull. It was small and weathered, with hollow eye sockets that seemed to stare back at them.

As soon as they picked up the skull, they heard a low moan emanating from the back of the barn. They tried to ignore it, but the sound grew louder and more insistent, until it was a deafening shriek that shook the very foundations of the barn.

The group tried to flee, but the door was jammed shut. They were trapped with the screaming skull, its terrifying shrieks echoing through the barn and piercing their skulls.

As the hours passed, the group began to feel different. They were hotter than before, and their skin seemed to be boiling. They screamed, but the skull's screeches drowned out their voices, and their pleas for help went unheard.

It wasn't until dawn broke that the skull's shrieks finally died down, leaving the group dazed and traumatized. They stumbled out of the barn, and the villagers who saw them were horrified by their appearance.

The group had been changed by the cursed skull, and they were never the same again. Their skin had turned a sickening shade of gray, and their eyes held an otherworldly glow.

The skull remained undisturbed, but its power continued to grow, its screams becoming more intense with each passing day. The villagers knew that they had to do something to contain the skull's power before it was too late.

In the end, they decided to seal the barn, with the screaming skull locked within. It remained there, a terrifying reminder of the dangers of disturbing objects that are best left untouched.

6. The Ghostly Bride of Thornton: A woman who died on her wedding day and whose ghost still wanders the corridors of an old hall in Thornton.

For centuries, the old hall in Thornton had been home to a terrifying presence - the ghostly bride of Thornton. She had died on her wedding day, but her spirit lingered on, doomed to spend eternity wandering the corridors of the hall.

No one knew the bride's true story, but legend had it that her fiancé had abandoned her at the altar. The shock and heartbreak had caused her to fall ill and die, with her ghost remaining trapped in the hall ever since.

Many had claimed to have seen the bride over the years, her spectral figure appearing in the darkness and her eerie wails echoing throughout the halls. But no one was ever brave enough to investigate further.

That was until one group of explorers decided to spend the night in the old hall, keen to capture evidence of the ghostly bride. They had equipped themselves with cameras and voice recorders, eager to uncover the truth behind the legend.

As soon as they entered the hall, they could feel a chill settling over them. They began to set up their equipment, determined to capture any evidence of the ghostly bride's presence.

Suddenly, they heard a strange noise coming from the corridor, and one of the members went to investigate.

As soon as they entered the corridor, they could feel a sense of dread spreading through them. The air was thick with the scent of flowers, and the sound of sobbing filled their ears.

They pointed their camera towards the source of the sound, and there, in front of them, was the ghostly bride of Thornton. She was clad in a tattered wedding dress, her hair hanging loose around her face.

The explorers tried to run, but the ghostly bride followed them, her mournful wails echoing through the halls. They found themselves trapped in the old chapel, with the bride standing before them, her eyes filled with fury.

As they watched in horror, the ghostly bride began to dissolve before their eyes, her screams echoing through the room. The sound was deafening, and the explorers knew that they had to do something before it was too late.

They barricaded the entrance to the chapel, hoping to contain the bride's ghost within. But nothing they did could silence her screams, which echoed through the halls for years to come.

The ghostly bride of Thornton remains trapped within the halls to this day. Her screams still haunt the visitors of the old hall, for those who dare to venture inside are never safe from the wrath of the bride.

MY STORY

The old hall in Thornton creaked and groaned under the weight of centuries of history. Many tales of tragedy and despair were said to haunt its stately rooms, but none were as harrowing as the story of the Ghostly Bride.

Centuries ago, on a sunny day in early summer, the halls of the ancient manor were swathed in flowers and music filled the air. It was to be a day of romance and love, the day when the young heiress of the manor was set to marry her childhood sweetheart.

The ceremony was beautiful, the bride a vision of loveliness in white satin and pearls. The guests were happy, the music playing and the banquet bounteous. The bride and groom were set to emigrate to America after the ceremony, where they would start a new life together, free from the expectations of her family.

As the day wore on, guests began to notice that the groom had disappeared. The bride grew increasingly anxious, waiting for the man she loved to appear. Hours passed, and still, there was no sign of the groom.

Just before midnight, a message arrived at the manor, delivered by a panting servant, his face twisted with trepidation. He told the bride that her groom had been arrested for theft and was already on his way to the hangman's noose.

The bride was heartbroken, but she knew that she could not abandon her beloved. She dressed hurriedly and set out on the road towards the execution site. The rain was torrential, and she was drenched to the bone by the time she arrived.

As she reached the scaffold, the executor's assistant handed her a small box. The bride opened the box and let out an ear-piercing shriek. The head of her beloved was inside.

Days after the gruesome discovery, the bride was found dead in the halls of the ancient manor. Her spirit, it is said, still roams those same halls, doomed to forever search for her missing groom.

Many claimed to have seen her, a tragic figure haunting the rooms, her mournful sobs echoing through the halls. Her ghostly shape appeared just before midnight, the time she had set out on that fatal journey.

Guests at the manor reported strange occurrences. They saw the ghost of the bride in a white dress standing at the edge of the bed, her long hair falling down over her face, or heard her whispering in their ears in the dead of night.

The ghostly bride of Thornton still walks the halls of the old hall, forever trapped in her grief and pain, searching for her beloved and waiting for the day she can be reunited with him in death.

7. The Phantom Coach of Oxenhope: A ghostly carriage that is said to race through the streets of Oxenhope, driven by a headless coachman and pulled by four black horses.

The streets of Oxenhope were said to be haunted by a terrifying presence - the Phantom Coach. Late at night, the sound of horses' hooves and creaking wheels could be heard, heralding the arrival of the ghostly carriage and its headless coachman.

Many had claimed to have seen the coach, its ghostly form rushing through the streets, the horses' breath streaming like smoke into the night air. But no one was ever brave enough to investigate further.

That was until one brave explorer decided to spend the night in Oxenhope, determined to capture evidence of the Phantom Coach. He equipped himself with a camera and headed out into the night.

As soon as he entered the dark streets, he could feel a chill settling over him. He began to set up his camera, determined to capture any evidence of the ghostly coach's presence.

Suddenly, he heard a strange noise coming from the end of the street, and he went to investigate. As soon as he turned the corner, he caught a glimpse of the Phantom Coach racing towards him.

The coach was pulled by four black horses, their eyes glowing red in the darkness. The coachman was headless, his body wrapped in a tattered cloak. The coach raced towards the explorer, the sound of the horses' hooves getting louder and louder.

The explorer tried to run, but the coach was too fast, bearing down on him with terrifying speed. He felt the cold breath of the horses on his back, and he knew that it was only a matter of seconds before the coach caught up with him.

Suddenly, the coach swerved to the side, narrowly missing the explorer. The coach continued down the street, disappearing into the darkness.

The explorer stumbled backwards, shaken by the near-miss. He knew that he had captured something extraordinary on his camera - evidence of the Phantom Coach of Oxenhope.

As he looked at the footage, he saw the coach racing towards him, the horses' breath streaming like smoke into the night air. He could hear the coachman's maniacal laughter, the sound of his voice chilling to the bone.

The Phantom Coach of Oxenhope remains a terrifying presence to this day. No one knows who its passengers are, or where it takes them, but it is said that whoever sees the coach will never be the same again, forever haunted by the sound of horses' hooves and the coachman's mad laughter.

MY STORYS
1ST STORY

The wind whistled through the narrow cobbled streets of Oxenhope, sending shivers down the spines of the few residents who dared to venture out at night. The sound of horses' hooves could be heard in the distance, growing louder and more frenzied by the second.

Suddenly, out of the darkness, emerged a ghostly carriage. It was the Phantom Coach of Oxenhope, its driver a headless coachman, and the horses pulling the carriage were four black stallions, their eyes glowing in the darkness like two bright red coals. The carriage rushed through the streets at breakneck speed, its wheels creaking and groaning with each turn.

The Phantom Coach had been haunting the streets of Oxenhope for centuries, and every night it appeared, it was with a renewed sense of terror for the residents.

The coach was said to be the transport of souls, those who had died tragically or who were doomed to wander the Earth for all eternity. They would be collected by the coachman, who would steer them through the streets of Oxenhope before disappearing into the night fog, never to be seen again.

One dark and stormy night, a young couple was driving home from a party, speeding on the narrow and winding road that led to Oxenhope. The young woman was driving, and the pair was arguing, though neither one of them could remember why.

As the car approached the outskirts of the town, they noticed something moving in the shadows. As they got closer, they saw the Phantom Coach of Oxenhope, racing towards them at full speed.

The woman tried to swerve off the road, but it was too late. The carriage hit their car head-on, sending them spinning out of control. When the car came to a stop, the couple found themselves stranded, stuck in the darkness with no one around to help them.

Suddenly, they heard the sound of horses' hooves, and the coach materialized out of the darkness. The couple could hear the ghostly laughter of the coachman, and then they heard the sound of a hand knocking on the glass of the passenger window.

The young woman looked up and screamed, for what she saw was the headless coachman, his face twisted in a gruesome grin, standing beside the car.

The young couple was never seen again, and to this day, the Phantom Coach of Oxenhope continues to haunt the streets and lanes of the small town – a terrifying presence that warns all who dare to venture out at night.

2ND STORY

The villagers whispered about it in hushed tones. They knew better than to talk too loudly about the Phantom

Coach of Oxenhope. But on this particular night, the silence was broken by the sound of hurried footsteps. A young man ran through the streets, his heart pounding in his chest.

The Phantom Coach was coming, and there was no stopping it.

The young man had heard the stories, of course, but he had never believed them. Until now. As he turned the corner, he saw the ghostly carriage hurtling towards him, driven by a headless coachman and pulled by four black horses.

Panic set in, and he turned to run, only to find that the streets had disappeared. In their place was a dense forest of gnarled trees, their twisted limbs reaching out like bony fingers. The sound of the coach's wheels grew louder and louder, and the young man was sure he was about to die.

But then, as if on cue, the trees parted, revealing an old, abandoned mansion.

The young man raced inside, slamming the door shut behind him. He was safe, or so he thought. For as soon as he looked up, he saw the headless coachman looming in front of him, his eyes glowing red.

But then something unusual happened, and the young man noticed that the coachman wasn't trying to hurt him. Instead, he was trying to tell him something.

Through his disfigured gurgles, the coachman told the young man that he had been cursed, that his soul could never rest until he completed his mission. That mission, he said, was to find someone who was pure of heart and brave enough to take his place as the coachman of the Phantom Coach.

The young man hesitated but then decided to take up the challenge. He climbed onto the driver's seat, and the four black horses took off at full speed.

For hours, the young man raced around the countryside, through the darkness of the forest and over the hills. He could feel the weight of the curse lifting, and as the first light of dawn began to break, the Phantom Coach came to a halt.

The young man stepped out of the carriage, the curse now lifted. The coachman turned to him, and for the first time, the young man saw kindness in his eyes.

And in that moment, the young man knew that he had broken the curse of the Phantom Coach of Oxenhope.

8. The Lady in Blue: The ghost of a woman who died of a broken heart and whose spirit still inhabits the ruins of an old abbey in Haworth.

The ruins of the old abbey in Haworth had always been a place of great mystery and intrigue. But for those who dared to venture inside, it was said that the ghost of the Lady in Blue still roamed the halls, her grieving cries echoing through the stone walls to this very day.

The Lady in Blue was once a beautiful woman, with piercing blue eyes that seemed to sparkle like diamonds. She had lived a charmed life, with riches and all the luxuries that money could buy.

But then she met the man she loved, a rugged and handsome young man with a heart of gold. They fell in love, and for a time, their love was all-consuming. But then, tragedy struck.

The Lady in Blue's lover died in a tragic accident, and his death broke her heart. She withdrew from the world, spending all her days and nights mourning the loss of her beloved. Eventually, she became so consumed with grief that she died alone in her chambers, her broken heart unable to withstand the pain any longer.

But even in death, her spirit refused to leave the abbey. It was said that she had been buried with her lover's cloak, which she wore all the time, becoming the Lady in Blue that roamed the halls.

Her cries could be heard throughout the ruins, and many have felt her ghostly presence. Those who did were overcome with an eerie sense of sadness, as if the Lady in Blue's grief and pain had somehow seeped into their very souls.

One particularly dark night, a group of adventurous teenagers journeyed to the abbey, eager to see if the stories were true.

As they made their way through the ruins, they heard her mournful cries growing louder and louder, and then without warning, the Lady in Blue appeared before them.

They could see the outline of her cloak, billowing in the wind, and they could hear her sobs, the sound of her heart still broken after all these years.

But then, one of the teenagers, a brave young woman with a heart of steel, stepped forward, offering the Lady in Blue the comfort and love she had been missing all these years.

And with one final cry, the Lady in Blue disappeared, her spirit finally able to rest as she let go of her grief and heartache.

But the memory of the Lady in Blue still lingers in the ruins of the old abbey, a reminder of the power of love and the devastating consequences of a broken heart.

9. The Specter of Haworth Parsonage: The ghostly presence that is felt by visitors to the parsonage where the Bronte sisters lived and wrote their famous novels.

The Haworth Parsonage was a place of great literary fame, known for being the home of the Bronte sisters, who had created brilliant works of fiction that truly immortalized them.

However, the parsonage had another claim to fame, something that the visitors and the Bronte sister themselves tried to keep a secret. The Specter of Haworth Parsonage was an ever-present ghostly presence, one that made the hairs on the back of your neck stand on end.

Many visitors claimed to have seen it, felt it, and even heard it, as if something still lingered in the hallways and rooms of the old house.

For some, it was just a feeling, a sense of unease and uneasiness that hung in the air, making them feel as though someone – or something – was watching them.

For others, it was much more than that. They claimed to see a figure, a dark shape that drifted through the halls, looking for something or someone.

Those who claimed to have seen the specter described it as having a pale, gaunt appearance, with sunken eyes and a thin-lipped mouth. It moved noiselessly, with a sense of otherworldly grace that suggested it was not quite alive.

Some of the girls had claimed that the specter of Haworth Parsonage was one of the Bronte sisters, returned to haunt the house where they had lived and died. Others suggested that it was something more malevolent, a dark force that had been drawn to the house by the fame and power of the Bronte sisters.

Whatever the true nature of the Specter of Haworth Parsonage, one thing was certain: it was an ever-present, ghostly presence that could never be entirely exorcized from the halls of the old house.

Even today, the specter remains, haunting the house where the Bronte sisters once lived and wrote their famous novels, a reminder of the dark and mysterious forces that dwell in the shadows of our imagination.

10. The White Lady of Ponden Hall: A spectral figure in white that is said to haunt the rooms of this ancient hall near Haworth.

Ponden Hall was an ancient house, cloaked in mystery, history and legends. For centuries, the people of Haworth spoke in hushed tones of The White Lady of Ponden Hall, the spectral figure that haunted the halls and rooms with her ghostly presence that no one could deny.

The White Lady was said to dress in flowing white robes, her hair and face hidden behind a veil of mist. According to local legend, she was a jilted lover who had taken her own life in the house after her lover had left her for another woman.

Many visitors to the house reported feeling her icy presence, as if she was watching them from behind the veil of mist. Some claimed to have seen her, wandering the halls and rooms as if searching for something or someone.

But it was in the attic room where the White Lady's presence was most profound. Many people had reported feeling a chill run down their spine as they entered the room, driven almost to the point of madness by the overwhelming sense of fear and terror that emanated from it.

On some rare occasions, visitors claimed to have seen the White Lady herself, standing in the shadows with her ghostly form shimmering in the faint light. They described her as a beautiful woman, pale and delicate with her hair flowing long and dark behind her.

But there was something about her that was undeniably unsettling, a sense of anger and injustice that clung to her like a shadow. It was as if she was still trapped in the moment of her own tragedy, unable to move on and find peace.

And so, visitors continued to flock to Ponden Hall, intrigued by the stories of The White Lady and the mystery that still surrounded her. Some came hoping to catch a glimpse of her ghostly form, while others cowered in fear, unwilling to test the truth of the local legend.

But no matter what they believed or hoped to find, there was no denying the undeniable truth – the White Lady of Ponden Hall was real, and her presence still lingered in the house after all these years.

MY STORY

The White Lady of Ponden Hall was a legend that had persisted for centuries. The spectral figure in white that haunted the ancient hall near Haworth was said to be the ghost of a woman who had been wronged by those she loved.

Many a tale had been spun around the White Lady, but it was the one about her love for a young man from a neighbouring estate that was the most tragic of them all. The young man had promised to marry her, but when his parents found out about their relationship, they forbade him from seeing her again.

Desperate and heartbroken, the young woman took her own life in the attic room of Ponden Hall.

But her spirit refused to leave the house, and she began to haunt the halls and rooms. Her ghostly presence could be felt by anyone who dared to enter, and her mournful cries could be heard in the still of night.

Countless housekeepers and caretakers had tried to exorcise the White Lady from the house, but nothing seemed to work. For years, she had been a part of the fabric of Ponden Hall.

And so, the family who owned the estate decided to open the house to the public. They believed that the White Lady's presence would be a drawcard, and it was. Visitors flocked to the ancient house in droves, hoping to catch a glimpse of the spectral woman.

But the White Lady had her own ideas. She didn't like all these people traipsing through the halls and rooms of her home. And so, she decided to make her presence known.

One evening, a young couple decided to stay overnight in the attic room where the White Lady had died. They had always been fascinated by ghost stories, and they had hoped to experience something paranormal during their stay.

But it was a decision that they would come to regret.

As they lay in bed, they heard a noise coming from the corner of the room. At first, they thought it was just the house settling, but then they heard it again. It was a muffled sob, the cry of a woman in pain.

And then they saw her – the White Lady of Ponden Hall. She stood at the foot of their bed, her ghostly form shimmering in the half-light. She was everything they had imagined and more, but her presence was terrifying.

The couple tried to run from the room, but the door wouldn't budge. The White Lady was blocking their exit, her dark eyes glaring at them from behind her veil of mist.

For hours they were trapped, hearing her plaintive cries, feeling her icy presence. And then, as suddenly as she had appeared, the White Lady disappeared, her ghostly form dissolving into the air.

The couple never went back to Ponden Hall, too terrified by what they had experienced. But they would never forget the White Lady, the spectral figure in white that haunted the halls of the ancient house near Haworth.

11. The Spooklight of Keighley Road: A mysterious light that has been reported by many motorists driving along Keighley Road, said to be a supernatural phenomenon.

The Spooklight of Keighley Road was an elusive and mysterious phenomenon that had been reported by many motorists for decades. It was said to be a supernatural occurrence, something that defied explanation and logic.

Many theories had been put forward to explain the Spooklight, but none of them seemed to hold water. Some claimed it was simply a car's headlights, reflecting off the trees and creating an optical illusion. But others had seen the Spooklight when there was no car in sight.

And then there were the stories that sent shivers down the spine. Tales of people who had seen ghosts standing by the side of the road, illuminated by the eerie light of the Spooklight, as if waiting for someone to pick them up and take them home.

Mary had heard these stories many times, but she had never given them much thought. She was a logical and rational person, and she knew that there was always a rational explanation for these things. But that was before she had her own encounter with the Spooklight.

It was a cold and dark night when Mary was driving home from work along Keighley Road. She was tired and ready for bed, but she still had a long way to go. And then she saw it – the Spooklight.

At first, she thought it was just a reflection from a car's headlights, but as she got closer, she realized that there was no car in sight. And that was when she saw it – the figure standing by the side of the road, illuminated by the eerie light of the Spooklight.

Mary's heart raced as she drew closer, unsure of what to do. Should she stop and help the person standing by the side of the road? Or should she drive on, knowing that the Spooklight was not something to be trifled with?

As she drew closer, Mary saw that it was not a person at all. It was a figure, a ghostly presence that seemed to shimmer in the light of the Spooklight. And then it disappeared, leaving Mary alone in the darkness of the night.

She tried to shake off the feeling of fear and dread that had settled over her, but the memory of the Spooklight and the ghostly figure standing by the side of the road would haunt her for years to come.

And so, the legend of the Spooklight of Keighley Road lived on, a reminder that some things in this world were not meant to be explained. Some things were simply meant to be experienced, whether we wanted to or not.

12. The Haunted Alleyway of Haworth: A narrow alleyway that is said to be cursed and haunted by the ghosts of the people who were buried alive there during the plague.

The Haunted Alleyway of Haworth was a place of dread and terror. Its narrow and winding path nestled between the ancient buildings of the town, and it was said to be cursed and haunted by the ghosts of the people who had been buried alive during the plague.

For centuries, the people of Haworth had avoided the alleyway, fearful of the horrors that lay within. Some claimed to have heard the sound of moans and muffled screams emanating from beneath the cobblestones. Others had reported seeing ghostly figures lurking in the shadows, their pale and emaciated bodies writhing in pain and agony.

But the truth was even more horrifying. During the peak of the plague, the alleyway had been used to bury the dead. But as the number of bodies grew, space became scarce. And so, the decision was made to bury the living with the dead, to let them die a slow and agonizing death beneath the earth.

It was a decision that would haunt the town for centuries to come.

The alleyway became known as the place where the living were buried with the dead, a cursed place where the spirits of the victims still roamed, their tormented souls trapped between this world and the next.

And then, one dark and stormy night, a group of foolish teenagers decided to explore the alleyway. They were bored and looking for a thrill, and the Haunted Alleyway of Haworth seemed like just the thing.

At first, it was just a game, something to pass the time. But then they heard it – a sound coming from beneath the cobblestones, a sound that chilled them to the bone.

And then they saw it – a ghostly figure standing at the end of the alleyway, its pale and emaciated body writhing in agony. The teenagers tried to run, but they found themselves trapped, their screams silenced by the sound of moans and muffled screams.

For hours they were trapped, the ghosts of the dead and dying surrounding them, their tormented spirits seeking revenge for the horrors that had been inflicted upon them.

And then, as suddenly as it had begun, it was over. The ghosts disappeared, leaving the teenagers alone and terrified in the darkness of the alleyway.

They never spoke of their experience again, too scared of what they had seen and heard. But the legend of the Haunted Alleyway of Haworth persisted, a reminder of the horrors that had been inflicted upon the innocent during the plague.

MY STORY

The Haunted Alleyway of Haworth was a place that a brave few dared venture. A narrow passage surrounded by old buildings, it was said to be cursed and haunted by the ghosts of the people who had been buried alive there during the plague.

The townspeople had sealed the alleyway years ago, hoping to trap the spirits within its walls forever. But the seal had been broken by time and weather, and the evil still lingered.

One night, a group of five old friends ventured into the alleyway. They had heard stories about the curse, but they didn't believe in superstition. They were looking for a thrill and an exciting adventure.

As they walked into the alleyway, they felt a strange force pulling them towards something they couldn't see. They tried to shake it off, but it grew stronger with every step.

Suddenly, they found themselves surrounded by the ghosts of the past. The ghosts looked at them with empty eyes, their skin pale and their bodies malnourished.

The friends were terrified. They tried to run back, but they found themselves trapped. It was as if the walls were closing in around them, sealing them in their fate.

The ghosts began to move closer to them, making the friends feel as though they were suffocating. Their screams filled the alley as they tried to escape the grip of the dead.

As if by some lucky twist of fate, one of the friends discovered an old relic, an exorcism book, tucked under his jacket. He'd brought it along as a joke or so he thought, yet now it seemed like it would prove useful.

The group huddled in a circle as the friend tried to recite the words of the exorcism. The ghosts seemed to be fighting back, their screams drowning out the chanting.

But the friends persisted, feeling the walls closing in on them. Suddenly, there was a powerful gust of wind, and the ghosts were gone, swept away by the force of exorcism.

The friends fell back, gasping for air, tears streaming down their faces. They knew they had been lucky this time. They would never forget the haunted alleyway of Haworth and the spirits that would forever remain cursed within.

13. The Ghosts of Weavers' Square: The spectral figures that are said to appear in this historic square on certain nights, leaving behind a sense of dread and unease.

Deep in the heart of Haworth, there is a historic square that has been home to the textile industry for generations. Known as Weavers' Square, the area is steeped in history and a dark legend of terror and despair.

The Ghosts of Weavers' Square are the spirits of the weavers who once worked in the mills. They are said to appear at certain times of the year on certain nights, leaving behind a sense of dread and unease.

The weavers were known for their hard work and dedication to the mills, but they were also mistreated and abused. They worked long hours in harsh conditions that caused them physical and emotional torment.

It's said that their souls, unable to find peace in death, still roam the square, seeking vengeance on those who wronged them in life.

Many people have reported seeing the Ghosts of Weavers' Square. Their misty, ethereal forms move and shift, giving the impression that they are still hard at work.

But, of course, no one dared to stay in the square after dark. The legends of the Ghosts of Weavers' Square were enough to keep locals and visitors alike avoiding the area entirely.

Once, a group of thrill-seekers dared to stay the night in the square, wanting to test out the legend. They scoffed at the stories and steeled themselves for what they believed to be a harmless ghost story.

But as the night wore on, the spirits took shape and started to move towards them. The teenage group tried to outrun them but it was no good. The ghosts took their revenge and engulfed the group.

The screams echoed throughout the town, and ever since that night, no one has dared to visit Weavers' Square after dark.

And so, the Ghosts of Weavers' Square continue to haunt the living, a dark reminder that the past has a way of catching up, and sometimes, the dead have a score to settle.

MY STORY

The Ghosts of Weavers' Square were a dark and haunting presence in the otherwise tranquil town. Legend had it that at certain times of the year, on certain nights, the spectral figures would appear.

It was said that the ghosts were the spirits of the weavers who had once lived and worked in the square.

They had been mistreated and abused, their bodies broken by the long hours and harsh conditions of working in the mills.

And now, their restless spirits roamed the square, seeking vengeance on those who had wronged them.

Many people claimed to have seen the ghosts, their misty forms drifting through the square. They left behind a sense of dread and unease, as if the very air had been poisoned by their presence.

But no one dared to explore the square after dark. No one wanted to risk encountering the ghosts of Weavers' Square.

One night, a group of teenagers were on a dare to spend the night inside the square. They were supposed to be back before dark, but they lost their sense of time and realized they were still in the square when night fell.

They watched as the weavers' ghosts started to take shape. Their eyes glowed with an otherworldly light as they moved towards the terrified teenagers who had nowhere to run.

One teenager tried to catch the attention of the ghosts, as if he wanted to communicate with them. They had a strange feeling that he had a connection with the ghosts but before they could find more, the ghosts engulfed them.

The screams echoed through the town as the weavers' spirits took their revenge. And so, the legend of the Ghosts of Weavers' Square lived on, a solemn reminder that not all spirits can be laid to rest, and sometimes, the past comes back for revenge. The town always remembered to keep out of the square after dark.

14. The Curse of Haworth Church: The strange occurrences and ghostly happenings that have been reported at the church in Haworth, believed to be the result of a curse placed on it centuries ago.

The Curse of Haworth Church is a story that has been etched into the fabric of the town. Centuries ago, it was said that a curse was placed on the church, and ever since then, the place has been plagued by strange occurrences and ghostly happenings.

Many people have reported hearing unexplained voices and footsteps echoing through the halls of the church. Others have felt a ghostly presence watching them from the shadows.

Legend has it that the curse was placed on the church by an angry witch who had been wronged by the town's people. Her spirit, enraged by the injustice done to her, vowed to take revenge on generations to come.

The witch's curse worked, and the church was enveloped in a malevolent force. It became a dark and foreboding place, feared by all who knew of its history.

Visitors to the church would often report feeling an ice-cold presence that caused the hair on their arms to stand on end. They would feel as if they were being followed by a ghostly figure, or as if the walls themselves were alive with an evil energy.

No one dared to stay in the church after dark. The pews, once a place of comfort and refuge, were now a place of terror and darkness.

Once, a group of teenagers decided to explore the church after dark. They scoffed at the stories of the curse, believing themselves to be invincible.

But they quickly found themselves lost in a maze of dark corridors, their flashlight flickering as if it was about to go out.

They heard whispers and otherworldly moans around them and saw a shadowy figure. Suddenly, they found themselves at the altar, standing before the witch's curse. The ghostly figure was upon them with icy breaths and they screamed in terror as they ran out of the church.

The Curse of Haworth Church continues to haunt the people, a dark reminder that sometimes, curses are real, and sometimes, the supernatural forces are beyond our understanding.

MY STORY

The old Haworth church was once a place of sanctuary, a beacon of faith that shone brightly across the town. But that all changed when the curse fell upon the stone walls, a malevolent force that would terrify all who entered.

No one quite remembers how the curse began, but the legend goes that an ancient witch who was wronged by the town's people placed it on the church.

From then on, the church became a place shrouded in darkness and fear. The people of Haworth stopped attending mass, and the church fell into ruin, its walls overgrown with weeds and ivy.

Yet, the curse remained, and those who dared to set foot on the grounds of the church after dark did so with bated breath and fearful hearts.

Many people claimed to have seen ghostly figures roaming the church grounds at night. Some reported hearing blood-curdling screams coming from the depths of the church, while others claim to have seen shadowy figures in the bell tower.

One autumn evening, Lily, a young woman who was new to the town, decided to explore the abandoned church. The town's people warned her against it, saying that the curse would find her, but she shrugged off their warnings.

As soon as the sun began to set, Lily set out towards the deserted church. As she got closer, she saw the gate to the graveyard swing open of its own accord. A chill ran down her spine as she entered the churchyard, and the hairs on the back of her neck stood on end.

She stepped inside the church, and the atmosphere changed. The air grew cold, and the shadows deepened.

She moved cautiously through the nave, feeling eyes watching her from every direction.

Suddenly, she heard a noise from the bell tower. She looked up to see a ghostly figure slip through the door. The figure was inhuman and ethereal, yet it seemed to be aware of her presence.

As the ghostly figure moved towards her, Lily ran across the church. She heard the doors close on their own and she was locked inside.

She tried to push against them, but they remained steadfast. She heard ghostly whispers surrounding her and she shrieked in terror.

For hours afterward, Lily remained locked in the church until the morning sun finally shone through the stained-glass windows of the church. From that day forward, she never ventured near the Haworth church again.

The Curse of Haworth Church is a nightmare that still grips the town, a potent reminder of the darkness that lurks within the shadows of our world.

The old church in Haworth was once a symbol of hope, a place where people could seek refuge and solace, but the curse changed everything, turning it into a place of horror and despair.

The curse began over three centuries ago when the church was built. It was said that a group of local witches had cursed the church, vowing to make it a place of suffering and pain.

As the years passed, the curse took hold of the church's walls, twisting and gnarling them until they resembled something out of a nightmare.

People who ventured into the church at night reported hearing terrible screams coming from the depths of the church. Others said they felt a cold breeze whispering through the halls, and some claimed they heard the sound of ghostly voices.

Many believe that the curse is still alive and well, punishing the living for the sins of their ancestors.

One dark and stormy night, a group of teenaged friends wandered into the church and dared each other to explore the building's inner sanctum. The wind howled against the walls as they made their way inside, flashlight in hand.

The church was eerily quiet as they crept through the darkened corridors. The only sound was their footsteps echoing through the halls.

As they entered the nave, the air grew colder, and the shadows deepened. They heard a strange moaning sound coming from above and looked up to see what appeared to be a ghostly figure.

It was a woman's figure with long hair, wearing a white gown. It hovered above them, unworldly and ethereal.

Suddenly, the building shook, and the walls creaked and groaned. The teens froze in terror as the ghostly figure turned its attention towards them. Its eyes glowed red, and they could feel its rage.

With a shriek, the ghostly figure hurtled towards them, and they ran for their lives. The floor beneath them cracked, and they tumbled through to an abandoned underground crypt.

From the crypt, they could feel it lurking above, waiting for them. The figure of the witch appeared, eyes ablaze with anger. Then, the room filled with light and the witch disappeared.

The teens scrambled to their feet, gasping for air. They stumbled out of the crypt and never returned to the cursed church again.

And so, the Curse of Haworth Church lives on, a perpetual torment, awaiting all those who dare to enter its walls.

15. The Poltergeist of Lumb Bank: A malevolent spirit that is said to be responsible for moving objects and causing disturbances in this historic mansion near Haworth.

Lumb Bank was a grand old mansion on the outskirts of Haworth, a place steeped in history and legend. It was said that the building was once used as a hideout for highwaymen, and that it was home to a particularly malevolent spirit.

The poltergeist in Lumb Bank was a force to be reckoned with, causing disturbances in the house by moving objects and throwing them across the room. It was said that the poltergeist could move even the heaviest furniture with a single touch, and that it was always at its strongest during the darkest and coldest nights.

People who stayed in the mansion said they felt a malevolent presence lingering in the halls. They heard strange noises coming from the adjacent rooms, and they felt as if they were being watched.

One night, a family arrived at the mansion, eager to explore its rich history. The parents and their two children settled into the grand old house, excited for their adventure.

As the night wore on, the poltergeist made its presence known, throwing objects across the room and rattling the doors. The family was terrified, huddled together in the bedroom, hoping the terror would soon end.

The parents tried to comfort their children, but they were too afraid to sleep. Suddenly, they heard a loud banging on the door and a chilling voice calling out their names.

The poltergeist had returned, and he seemed more sinister than ever before. The family hugged each other tightly, hoping to survive the night.

With a deafening sound, the door burst open, and the poltergeist entered the room. It was a formless shadow, wreathed in a thick fog that seemed to suck everything into it.

The family screamed as the poltergeist approached them, reaching out to devour them. But then, a miracle occurred.

A beam of light flashed through the room, and the figure of a man appeared. He was clad in white robes, and his face was kind and welcoming.

"Be gone, evil spirit," the man commanded, and the poltergeist vanished with a shriek.

The family was safe, but they never forgot the terror of Lumb Bank. The mansion remains a place of mystery and intrigue to this day, and it is said that the poltergeist still lurks there, waiting for its next victim.

Final thoughts

The legends of Haworth are a testament to the human fascination with the supernatural. They speak of a world beyond our understanding, a place of spirits and demons that lurk in the shadows.

The curse of Haworth Church and the poltergeist of Lumb Bank are just two examples of the mysteries that surround the area. They remind us that there is much we do not know about the world, and that there are forces that we cannot control.

But they also remind us that there is hope. That even in the face of terror, there are those who stand up against the darkness and win.

The stories of Haworth will continue to fascinate and terrify people from all over the world, but they are also a reminder that life is precious, and that we should never take it for granted.

The world is a strange and mysterious place, but it is also full of wonder and beauty. Let us cherish the good, and stand united against all that threatens to destroy us.

For when the night falls, there will always be those who are willing to fight for the light. And in that battle against the darkness, there is hope for a better tomorrow.

Thank you for reading

Thank you for joining me on this journey through the haunted legends of Haworth. I hope that these tales have chilled you to the bone, and that they have left you with a sense of wonder and terror.

The world is a strange and terrifying place, but it is also full of beauty and mystery. From the cursed church of Haworth to the malevolent poltergeist of Lumb Bank, the stories of this area are a testament to the darker side of human existence.

But they are also a reminder that even in the face of horror, there is always hope. And it is that hope that drives us forward, that gives us the courage to face the unknown.

So thank you for reading, and may the spirits of Haworth continue to haunt you in your dreams.

Printed in Great Britain
by Amazon

34035762R00059